LEAVE THIS HOUSE

The frightening true story of the Birmingham poltergeist

By
Lee Brickley

Copyright @ Lee Brickley 2022

CONTENTS:

Introduction..5

The Letter..7

The Photograph..17

The Little Boy...25

The Sickness..35

The Possession...45

The Seance...56

The Old Man..67

The Truth...77

The Confrontation......................................87

The Peace..95

Afterword...101

INTRODUCTION

I have been fascinated with instances of poltergeist activity my entire life, and while most folks can go from cradle to grave without ever stumbling across something so unusual; I suppose it is only logical that a paranormal investigator like myself would end up at the centre of such phenomena eventually. Being a "real-life ghostbuster" often means I am the only helpful point of contact for those desperate people who fail to find understanding and assistance through traditional means, and that's pretty much how I became involved in the Birmingham poltergeist case back in 2021.

Imagine knives and other cutlery fly through the air in your kitchen, or taps turn on by themselves and flood your entire home. Picture a situation where you hear knocking coming from inside the walls and your valuables disappear and reappear as if by magic. It's possible you might call the police for help, but those well-meaning coppers rarely offer any support to families experiencing torment at the hands of evil spirits. That is why those in need are increasingly turning to me.

The Birmingham poltergeist case is by far the most extreme occurrence of otherworldly activity I have investigated during my decade-long career, and this is the first time I've ever written about it publicly. The names of the family involved in this case have been changed to protect their identities, but all the events described in this book are true- no matter how unbelievable that may seem to readers who weren't there.

Guy Lyon Playfair who investigated the famous Enfield Poltergeist case once told me that it was a life-changing experience and he would never forget it. I can honestly say the same thing about the story you are about to read. When you see these things happening with your own eyes and you encounter the presence of something quite so wicked and unholy, it's hard to go back to normal. None of the family will ever be the same again, and neither will I.

Grab yourself a hot chocolate, pull the blanket up over your head and get comfortable.

This is definitely going to freak you out!

THE LETTER

I awoke on 1st October 2021 with a peculiar ringing in my left ear. I heard it the second I opened my eyes, and the sound remained inside my head continuously all morning. It was a most peculiar thing. Both annoying and uncomfortable in equal measure, and after a couple of hours of torment, I'd had just about as much as I was going to take. I'd never suffered anything similar in the past, and so I thought it wise to call my doctor and make an appointment.

Standing up from the old, comfortable armchair in my living room, I began to slowly make my way into the hall to retrieve my mobile phone. It was at that moment I looked out of the window and saw the postman's familiar red jacket moving towards my house. The ringing in my ear intensified to the point where all I could do was place both hands on my head and squeeze my eyes closed hard.

The pain was becoming unbearable, but I opened my eyes again just in time to see the letterbox swing open and a single letter slide through. I watched as the envelope revealed itself and then floated down to the floor. As it came to rest, the pain in my head, and the ringing in my ears, seemed to disappear in unison. Transfixed on the letter, and feeling rather curious as to what just happened and why the noise in my ears seemed to have gone away, I reached down and carefully picked the envelope up with both hands.

As most people reading this book will know, I've been a full-time paranormal investigator for more than a decade now, and I've spent time investigating many different cases of supernatural activity, but what you probably don't know is how I sort through the masses of emails and letters I receive to determine which are genuine and worthy of my attention.

Well, I'll let you in on a little secret because my method is highlighted perfectly by this story. The truth is, I just get a feeling. Sometimes it's a tingling sensation at the back of my head, other times it might be butterflies in my stomach or a sudden rush of anxiety. In the case of the Birmingham poltergeist, it was the symptoms described above, and I realised the ringing in my ears was simply my intuition firing on all cylinders the second I opened the envelope and read the following letter:

Dear Mr Brickley,

I am writing this letter because I don't know what else to do. For more than a week now something has been trying to scare and maybe even hurt my family and I'm terrified because it seems to be getting worse every single night. I will try to explain everything so you understand what's happening. Please read this with an open mind. I would have thought a person was insane if they told me this a week ago, but I promise everything in this letter is real, and it's serious. My family desperately needs your help.

Eight days ago I bought a wooden photo frame from a charity shop on Erdington high street. It looked like it was empty, but when I got home and opened it up to remove the white card inside, it turned out there was an old photograph underneath of an angry-looking man. His eyes freaked me out so I threw the picture in the bin. Then I put the empty photo frame on a table and thought nothing else of it.

The following morning I was getting the kids ready for school (we have two girls), when I looked over towards the table in my kitchen and saw the photograph back inside the frame with the weird guy just staring at me again. I asked the girls if they'd taken the photo out of the bin but they both denied it and so did my husband later that night. I thought perhaps I was going mad and I hadn't even thrown the picture away in the first place, so I did it again.

I forgot all about it until I arrived home from work the next evening, but there it was again. As soon as I stepped through the door and walked into my kitchen, the man in the photograph with piercing eyes looked straight at me. I was convinced someone was playing a trick on me, and I gave my girls and my fella a real grilling that night, but they stuck to their guns and told me they had nothing to do with it.

I wanted to make sure the photograph went away and didn't come back this time, and I didn't want there to be any chance someone could be messing with me, so I put it in the wheelie bin outside late at night and then placed a full black bag of rubbish on top. I didn't tell anyone, and so I thought that would be the end of the matter, but I was wrong.

I walked downstairs in the morning to see the backdoor of our house wide open and the photo back in the frame. It was freezing. God knows how long the door must have been open. Not only that, but there was a trail of rubbish leading from the floor near the photograph, across the kitchen, and out of the open door.

I followed the trail of bottles, boxes, and wrappers all the way *down the side of our house to the wheelie bin at the bottom of the driveway. The lid was open, and it honestly looked as though someone covered in rubbish had climbed out of it and walked up our entryway and into the kitchen, all the while brushing themselves down and leaving a mess. I was petrified. I ran inside to check on the girls and tell my husband what had happened. He looked around to see for any signs of forced entry but couldn't find anything so we decided to talk about it more that evening.*

My husband suggested that we burn the photograph so that it would be impossible for it to get back in the frame in our kitchen. We burned it in a bucket in the garden and we were both sure that would be the end of it. Like clockwork though, that horrible face was back in the frame when I woke up the next day. No matter what we do, it just keeps coming back! Even if I move the picture frame into a different room, it's back in the kitchen every morning.

Now other things have started to happen that are really scaring the girls. We keep hearing loud bangs coming from the loft. My husband did take a look up there, but he couldn't see anything. You might think this sounds crazy, but we've also heard scratching coming from behind a wall in one of my daughter's bedrooms, and last night I watched a penny roll across the laminate floor in our living room. It seemed to come out of nowhere. My husband is working nights at the moment, and the girls were in bed. There's other stuff too.

I know your time is valuable, and I know you probably get a lot of strange people contacting you, but we're a normal family from Birmingham that would never make something like this up. I'm scared of telling my friends or anyone else for that matter because of what they might think, but the activity in our house is getting worse and I'm really worried something bad is going to happen. Please, please, contact me on the number below and tell me what I need to do to get you here. You're our only hope.

Yours faithfully,

Christine Evans
07********

After reading the rather unusual story from Mrs Evans, I decided to get straight on the phone. Time was clearly of the essence if this was a genuine case of ongoing paranormal activity, and I didn't want to waste a single moment. I dialled the number and it rang no more than twice before I heard a rather sheepish voice at the other end of the line say "hello?"

That phone call lasted for around forty-five minutes, which was precisely the amount of time it took for me to work out that Mrs

Evans was genuine in her request for assistance. At the very least, I was certain she believed she was telling me the truth, and that her circumstances meant it would be a very strange lie that would present her with no benefits or reward.

Mrs Evans was a respected primary school teacher, and her husband a building manager for a rather large West Midlands-based company. Neither of them held a particular belief in the paranormal before these events began and they were, by all accounts, rather embarrassed about it all. Mrs Evans certainly didn't want to publicise the happenings in any way or profit from the story, she just wanted the frightening events to stop.

I wrote down the family's address, which was in an area of Erdington called Gravelly Hill, and agreed to be there at 6pm the same evening. As is standard procedure, I packed my electronic equipment and some spare clothes into the car in case things turned sour and I had to pull an all-nighter. Little did I know that after arriving at the Evans' house, I wouldn't leave again for more than a few hours in almost two weeks. Indeed, I would soon find myself at the very heart of arguably the most horrifying poltergeist haunting the British Isles has ever known.

What I witnessed in that house changed me forever, and it changed the whole Evans family too, especially their eldest daughter Maggie. That little girl will have to live her entire life with the memory of these events etched into her brain, and that has to be more than the average child can handle. Who knows what long-term effects might manifest when you stare pure evil in the face at such a young age? More about that later though.

As promised, I pulled into the driveway of the Evans' house at precisely six-o'clock. It was a rather large home by today's standards, situated along Minstead Road near the famous Spaghetti Junction around three miles outside of Birmingham city centre. I could see Mrs Evans eagerly waiting at the window of the house as I stepped out of my car, and she bolted towards the front door which swung open with force long before I had any chance to knock.

"Thank God you're here" she shouted in a desperate tone. "It's happening now."

I asked Christine to explain what was going on as she quickly ushered me inside the house, but the woman could barely get a sentence out before the nature of the problem became abundantly clear. I was only two feet inside her kitchen when a bread knife seemed to appear out of nowhere and fly right past my face before crashing into the wall. A few seconds later, one of the cupboard doors started to open and close repeatedly causing a loud banging noise and making us both jump out of our skins. Out of sheer panic, my eyes scanned the room looking for more activity, and that was the first time I saw the infamous photograph sitting on a small family dining table. As my eyes met the eyes of the man in the picture, who looked just as Christine's letter had described, all the commotion seemed to stop, and things went eerily quiet for a moment. .

As the room fell silent I turned to Christine, who looked to be in a state of shock, and said the only words my brain could muster in that particular moment…

"I think we'd better put the kettle on."

THE PHOTOGRAPH

I sat for more than an hour drinking coffee with Christine and her husband John while their daughters Maggie and Emily watched cartoons. We talked extensively about the strange events happening in their home, and how the intensity of these seemingly paranormal occurrences seemed to be increasing. John didn't appear to be as worried as Christine, but as he explained, working the night-shift meant he was largely out of the house during the disturbances, and so they were having a much more damaging impact on his wife and daughter.

John was a tall man, probably around six and a half feet, and he had the sort of broad shoulders you only see on construction workers and WWE wrestlers. He wasn't a guy anyone would mess with in a hurry, and as first impressions go, he made a good one. John was clearly a man who cared about his family, it was just that he felt a little helpless in this situation. I promised John I'd do everything I could to work out what was going on and find a solution that allowed everyone to live a normal life again.

I asked Christine for more information about the photograph in the kitchen and she explained again that the purchase was accidental, and that she only meant to buy the nice old wooden frame. Christine told me it cost her five pounds from the British Heart Foundation shop on Erdington high street, and that she'd already been in touch with the shop to ask if they knew of the frame's previous owner so she could ask them about the photograph. Unfortunately, the staff at the shop had no idea.

During our chat, I learned that the Evans' oldest daughter Maggie had just turned twelve years old on 20th September, and their youngest girl Emily was soon to begin primary school a month or so later than she should have done at the age of four. That was because she had been very unwell with fevers at the beginning of September when the rest of her class took their morning registration for the first time, although the little girl was doing much better now.

I asked if John and Christine could gather the girls so I could speak to the whole family together, and they duly agreed. Maggie and Emily were such lovely children with permanent smiles on their faces. They were clearly well-looked after by their parents, and both were more than happy to entertain my questions.

I wanted to know what each of the girls had experienced so far, and they told me about loud bangs coming from the loft for a few days, and the weird scratching noise which seemed to resonate from a wall in Maggie's bedroom. Maggie sparked my curiosity further during her explanation when she told me that the scratching would get louder and louder until she told it to stop. When she said those words out loud, the scratching would go away instantly.

I asked the girls what they thought about the photograph of the scary man in their kitchen, and the elder sister said she was too frightened to even look at it, let alone pick it up and use the image to play tricks on her mother. The younger sister, Emily, seemed to go a little shy and initially refused to answer. Following some encouragement from her parents, the little girl said "that's my friend's daddy, but he's really mean."

Both Christine and John looked shocked. They asked their daughter to explain how she knew the man in the photograph and which friend he was related to. Emily told us she made her new friend a couple of days ago, and that he was a little boy. John said that was impossible as his daughter hadn't been outside the house for days, and she hadn't met any other children for much longer than that. It was then that Emily stunned the whole room into silence with the words "no daddy, my friend lives here."

John stood up and said that was enough for one night, and then began to get the children ready for bed while I ventured into the kitchen with Christine. She picked the wooden picture frame up, looked at the photograph for a moment, and then handed it to me. There really was something malevolent about the person in the image. When I held the photo in my hand and looked into the evil eyes of the unknown man, I could sense something was about to happen. It was at that moment Christine and myself heard John shouting for us from the upstairs landing.

I ran into the living room of the house and up the stairs as quickly as I could to find Mr Evans with an ashen complexion. "You look like you've seen a ghost," I said, attempting and failing to be humorous. John looked like he was about to have a panic attack, but with some calming words from myself and Christine, he began to open up.

John said he was just in the bathroom with Emily brushing her teeth when he saw a shadow move past the door on the landing. The protecting father left his daughter to take a look, and when he peered around the door, he saw what appeared to be a small child run into Emily's bedroom. That's when he shouted and we came running.

Not wanting to waste an opportunity to encounter an entity, I instantly walked towards the bedroom door which violently slammed shut with my face only a couple of inches away. I reached down for the handle and opened the door, then reached around with my other hand to find the light switch. I flicked the switch and the room lit up, but it seemed to be empty. Looking under the bed and inside the wardrobe, I found nothing more than mountains of toys and clothing. Whatever John saw wasn't there now. Little Emily became a little anxious because of all the commotion, and so it was decided she would sleep in her sister's bedroom for the night.

John read both of his daughters a bedtime story and kissed them on the forehead before turning out the light. At their request, the bedroom door was left slightly ajar, and the landing light stayed on. Myself, Christine, and her husband then descended back down the stairs and sat in the lounge for five minutes before John announced it was time for him to leave for work. He asked if I would be kind enough to stay the night and look after his family. I jumped at the chance as there had already been so much supernatural activity that I was certain we would experience more. I also wanted to set up some equipment and see if I could capture images or film of anything impressive.

The next few hours seemed to fly by as Christine told me all about her challenging job and how she met the love of her life

John when they were only teenagers. They really did seem like a lovely family, and I found myself feeling very sympathetic. All these strange happenings were definitely taking a toll on their lives, and I became even more determined to help them out.

It was three minutes past midnight when the next activity began. I had set up thermal imaging cameras and sound recording equipment all around the house, and I was sitting at the kitchen table monitoring everything from my laptop.

First there was a single bang that shook the entire house. It was so loud Christine was convinced one of the girls must have fallen out of bed and so she went off to check on them. I watched her walk up the stairs and across the landing on two thermal imaging cameras, and everything seemed normal. Around ten seconds later, there was another loud noise. I looked at the video on my laptop screen to see Christine running out of the bedroom in which her children were sleeping. The only thing was, this time she wasn't alone. There was another smaller figure on the thermal imaging screen that I presumed must have been her daughter Emily.

I walked to the bottom of the stairs and saw Christine standing at the top looking towards the loft hatch. She told me the second noise definitely came from above the girls' bedroom, and I asked if they were both okay. She informed me that her daughters were sound asleep and the booming sounds hadn't woken them. "Then who was that walking out of their room with you?" I asked.

Mrs Evans assured me there was nobody with her, but when I explained what I saw on the thermal imaging video, she went back into the children's' bedroom to check. Thankfully, all seemed calm, and both girls were still asleep. As Christine walked back towards me, another loud thud came from the loft above our heads followed immediately by a series of knocks in the following pattern:

Knock, Knock
Knock, Knock, Knock,
Knock, Knock,
Knock, Knock, Knock.

The pattern repeated exactly ten times. I wasn't counting as it happened as I spent the time attempting to work out where the noise was coming from. It seemed different to the bangs from the loft, more like it was coming from the walls inside the main part of the house, but it stopped before I found the precise location of its origin. The sound recordings from my microphones picked everything up, and so I was able to listen back to the audio with

Christine later on to determine the pattern and the frequency of the knocks.

Something weird happened while we were listening to those recordings. At the exact point the knocking ended on the sound file, my laptop froze and then turned itself off; something that had never once happened in the past. When I reached over to turn it back on, my hand brushed the wooden photo frame on the kitchen table which sent it crashing down to the floor. Mrs Evans looked at me intensely as I reached down and picked it up. Thankfully it wasn't broken.

I opened the back of the frame, removed the photo of the old man and turned it around before putting it back inside. I then explained to Christine that I would like to see what would happen if I locked the frame in my car overnight. Although hesitant, she agreed to my experiment, and so I went and locked the item in my glove-box.

There wasn't any more unusual activity that night, and so we both decided to turn in at around two o'clock in the morning. Christine offered me the sofa, which luckily folded out into a double bed. After the night I'd had, you might think I would find it difficult to sleep, but if you want to know the truth; I slept like a baby...at least until my car alarm started going off at sunrise.

THE LITTLE BOY

It was ten minutes to six o'clock in the morning when I heard the sound of my car alarm ringing out on the driveway of the Evans' house. I can't say how long it was going off before it disturbed my slumber, but I know it must have been less than twenty minutes. The particular alarm system on my vehicle will cut-out after that amount of time, but it was still very much in full-swing when I woke up that morning.

I jumped up from the sofa bed and threw my black t-shirt over my head. Within seconds, my jeans were buttoned-up and my socks were on. I ran for the kitchen to find it deserted with the backdoor of the house wide open. My eyes scanned the room, and I quickly noticed the seemingly "haunted" photo frame was back on the table as if it had never moved. Incredibly, the spooky photograph had turned itself back around in the frame and was once again facing outwards. I was astonished.

I reached into my pockets to check my car keys were still there and nobody could have stolen them during the night to access my car. They were still there, and with the sound of my car alarm now giving me a headache, I quickly ventured out of the front door and down the driveway. The state in which I found my car was somewhat unbelievable. All four doors were wide open, as was the boot and the bonnet. I walked around the car to see the petrol cap was open, and when I looked inside I noticed the glove-box was also down.

After closing everything up, I walked back inside the Evans' house to see Christine standing in the kitchen making a cup of coffee. She turned and noticed the photo had returned to the table."It came back again then?" She said looking rather unsurprised. I told her about the door being open and explained how I found my car, and Mrs Evans asked if I managed to catch anything on film. Unfortunately. I had made somewhat of a schoolboy error when setting up the thermal imaging cameras the previous evening. I positioned them to cover every room of the house except the kitchen because that's where I monitored the feeds. I would correct that mistake today and hopefully catch something next time.

Christine called the girls down for their breakfast at around the same time their father John returned home from work. The whole family sat down together, and I had a few minutes to quiz the girls over anything they might have seen or heard the previous evening. Maggie said she slept well but woke up a few times throughout the night feeling dizzy. She said she still felt dizzy this morning, and after taking her temperature, John decided it was best for her to spend the day in bed. It was a Saturday, and so resting wouldn't do the child any harm.

When Maggie left the breakfast table, her little sister Emily quickly tugged on my shirt and pulled me down so my ear was closer to her mouth. "The little boy was here again last night," she said quietly so her parents couldn't hear. I asked how she knew, and the shy Evans' girl said he came into her room as she was falling asleep because he wanted to play. Thrilled she was opening up to me, I asked Emily what game the little boy enjoyed, and she told me he always wanted to play hide and seek, but that last night he was very scared about something. She didn't know any more, but I asked her to come and get me the next time the little boy made an appearance.

John made sure his daughter Maggie was comfortable and resting in bed before he turned in for the day. With dark bags under his eyes, it was clear the night shift was taking its toll on the loving father. The whole family tried to remain as quiet as possible for the next few hours so as not to wake John. I used the time to make notes about all the events that had happened so far, and I also installed a motion-sensor thermal imaging camera in the kitchen.

Christine went upstairs to check on Maggie from time to time, and although she was sleeping, the little girl had a rather high temperature, and so her mother was becoming increasingly worried. She was overly cautious about these types of things because her other daughter Emily had only just overcome a bout of fever of an unknown origin. The woman was rightly concerned that Maggie might come down with the same mysterious illness.

At five o'clock in the evening, I heard John climb out of bed, walk across the landing, and lock himself in the bathroom, presumably to have a shower. Five minutes later, his youngest daughter Emily came running down the stairs and into the kitchen looking excited. "The little boy is here!" She shouted to me eagerly. "Show me," I said with just as much excitement as I got up from the kitchen chair. Emily proceeded to lead the way as we both went back upstairs and into her bedroom. Christine was doing some ironing on the landing at the time, and she came with us to see what was happening.

Emily pushed her bedroom door open and told me the little boy was in her room somewhere, but they were playing hide and seek and so he needed to find him. I walked around the room with the girl looking behind her curtains, in her toy box, and under the bed while her mother waited in the doorway. "He doesn't seem to be here," I said to the excited little girl with a slight look of disappointment on my face. Emily reassured me that the boy definitely was there, but he was just very good at hiding.

I sat down on Emily's bed and asked her to keep looking for the boy. I then turned my head to face her mother who was standing in the doorway observing all the proceedings. My stomach instantly felt weird and the hairs stood straight up on the back of my neck, as just for a split second, I saw a child peering at me from behind Christine's legs in the hallway. The little boy saw me, made eye contact, and then ran across the landing and out of view. It all happened so fast, but I shot up from the bed and almost knocked Christine over as I ran past her and onto the landing. As I did, John opened the bathroom door which violently shut in his face before he could walk through it.

Searching for the little boy, I swung every door open in the upstairs of the house, but he was nowhere to be found. I was now 100% convinced we were dealing with some kind of spirit. I had thought it was possible there might actually be a small child sneaking into the house, but it would have been impossible for a flesh and blood human to evade me in such a way. I checked every hiding place, but the boy was gone.

All the commotion caused a lot of panic, and so I decided to take Christine, John, and Emily downstairs to discuss what had just happened. Before we went down there, both parents checked in on their daughter Maggie, who was awake, but still feeling dizzy and completely unaware of the events that had just occurred. We left her to rest.

Downstairs I told Christine and John that I saw the little boy from Emily's stories, and that I believed they genuinely had a spirit in their home. Although I admitted that I was at a loss as to why the ghost of a happy child would cause poltergeist activity. I tried to describe the boy as much as possible, but as I only saw him for a second, I couldn't give many details. He was about three-feet tall. He wore old fashioned clothing, maybe from the early 1900s, and he looked to be from a working class background. I drew some similarities between the appearance of the entity and the way children are dressed in the hit Birmingham-based TV series Peaky Blinders. Or one could perhaps even say he looked a little like young Michael Banks from the classic Mary Poppins film.

John spoke up and asked about the photo in the kitchen. He said surely the man in the picture must have something to do with the disturbances as well. Otherwise, he reasoned, why would it be impossible to dispose of it? And why would it reappear on the table every time anyone tried? I told the worried father that I didn't have any answers for him just yet, but I was learning more with every minute that passed.

It was then that little Emily offered her piece to the conversation. At four years old, listening to her speak about the paranormal things happening in her home with such calmness was always a little spooky, but as I was fast learning, she seemed incredibly perceptive and intuitive. The youngest Evans' girl proceeded to tell her mother, father, and myself that the man in the kitchen was bad, and the little boy had been hiding from him for a long time. She said the little boy was scared that the bad man would find him soon. Emily then went back to playing with her toys on the living room floor leaving all the adults stunned once more.

We all heard a loud bang come from the upstairs of the house at precisely eight o'clock in the evening and quickly ran towards Maggie's room. The elder Evans' sister had been rather quiet for a couple of hours, and I presumed she was sleeping. As myself, John, and Christine burst through their daughter's bedroom door, we saw the girl lying on her bed looking panicked. "I can't move!" She screamed out in terror as her father ran towards the bed. "I can't move!" She shouted again.

John knelt down at the side of the bed and made myself and Christine aware that Maggie had something around her neck. Her father wrestled to loosen what appeared to be some kind of ligature that was tied around her throat, and after a few seconds, managed to rip it away. Maggie jumped up from the bed and ran into her mother's arms. "There was someone in here mommy," the frightened girl said as Christine held her tight. I began searching the room in an attempt to find anything of interest, but whatever was there had left. John put a piece of fluffy material in my hand and told me it was the rope-belt from Maggie's dressing gown. He said that was what was strangling her when we walked into the room. The weird thing was, it didn't have any knots in the belt, and yet John had to fight hard to loosen it and save his daughter. It was as if someone had placed it around the girl's throat while she was lying down in bed, lay themselves under the bed, and then pulled on each side of the belt until it was tight and choked her.

I told the whole family to grab some duvets and pillows and that we would all spend the rest of the night together in the living room. It seemed like a good idea as the girls would think it fun to have a sleepover with their parents, and John and Christine could keep a close eye on them.

Everyone went downstairs and I remained in Maggie's room for a while. I began to hear a scratching sound coming from behind her bedroom wall, and as the girl described to me the previous evening, it gradually became louder and louder. Testing out Maggie's method for making it go away, I simply told the noise to stop, and it did. Incredible!

I exited Maggie's bedroom and rejoined the Evans' family downstairs, who were all sitting on the same sofa hugging each other tightly. It was clear to see that Maggie was in bits. She was traumatised by her experience and the fact she nearly choked to death, and I just kept thinking how lucky it was that we found her when we did. I attempted to calm everyone down by telling them I would go and check the thermal footage to see if I'd managed to capture anything, but that didn't seem to make much difference. They were now scarred for their lives, and to be honest, so was I.

I just couldn't help but wonder how these events all fitted together. It seemed we were definitely dealing with the ghost of a small boy in the upstairs of the home, and he was communicating in some way with the Evans' youngest daughter Emily. It also appeared to be the case that the man in the photograph in the kitchen was the boy's father, and the child was hiding from him. It all seemed so confusing. I checked the thermal imaging footage to see it had managed to catch absolutely nothing, and so I sat awake with the family all night watching films. There were numerous more loud bangs coming from upstairs that evening, but we were all so scared that we chose to ignore them. Thinking back, I'd say we were all in a state of shock, but that was nothing. Things were about to get a lot worse!

THE SICKNESS

The next morning myself and the whole Evans' family woke to the sound of my car alarm going off once again. I was a little confused as I hadn't moved the photograph from the kitchen the previous night, and so I could think of no reason the alarm would be making such a noise. John said we'd better go check it out, and so we left Christine and the girls and ventured outside.

Unlike the previous morning, we did not find any of my car's doors open, but there was something unusual we both noticed as soon as we got close to the vehicle. There was a brown substance smeared all over my windscreen, probably mud, and within the smear there appeared to be some kind of writing.

I looked at John and he looked at me. Both of us were speechless as we saw the words "LEAVE THIS HOUSE " clearly written on the dirty glass. We didn't have time to find our words as we heard screams that John instantly knew belonged to his wife.

John and I ran back into the house as fast as we could to find both of his daughters looking scared on the sofa. We heard Christine scream again from upstairs and both bolted towards the staircase. "Maggie's room!" Christine shouted as we reached the landing. Her husband hit the door so hard to open it that I'm honestly surprised it didn't fly off its hinges, but panic was in the air, and this man's wife sounded as though she was in trouble.

As the door swung open, myself and John were greeted with the sight of Christine on her knees in the middle of the room holding her throat. The bedroom felt cold, and it looked different somehow. It was then I noticed the writing on the walls. Each of the four walls of the Evans' youngest daughter's room was now covered in writing. The phrase looked as though it was written in crayon, and it must have been repeated ten thousand times "LEAVE THIS HOUSE." It was exactly the same as the message on my car.

Christine caught her breath and then quickly informed us that something had been in the room with her, and all that writing wasn't on the wall a couple of minutes ago. The terrified mother told us how she had gone into Maggie's bedroom to get some clean blankets from the wardrobe, but when she walked through the door, it slammed behind her and wouldn't open. She said there was a rancid smell, and someone put their hands around her throat and began to strangle her from behind. All the while she could hear the words "LEAVE THIS HOUSE" being repeated over and over in some low, unearthly tone. Christine believed she passed out for a moment, and the words were all over the bedroom wall when she regained consciousness. All this had happened in the space of around a minute.

I advised John and Christine that it would be sensible to avoid Maggie's room and perhaps even fit a lock to the door until we could work out what was going on. John agreed and led his wife back downstairs to the girls, who wanted to know what had been happening. Their mother and father played the events down, but they told both Maggie and Emily they were not allowed into that particular bedroom for the time being.

Maggie was still looking a little worse for wear, and so Christine decided to take her temperature. The poor girl was still over thirty eight degrees, which would usually mean she should be taken to a hospital. However, the parents knew their daughter had a higher than average baseline temperature when she was well and healthy, and so they decided to hold out and see if the sickness would go away. Sadly, it didn't.

The eldest Evans' daughter became more and more ill as the day progressed. By the evening time, Maggie could do nothing more than lay on the sofa and sleep with her family around her.

Christine used a bag of frozen peas wrapped in a tea towel in an attempt to keep her little girl's temperature down, and that seemed to have at least somewhat of a positive effect.

At around six o'clock in the evening, I decided to sit down at my laptop and review the thermal imaging footage from Maggie's bedroom at the time Christine had her experience. I hadn't done it earlier as I was beginning to think the cameras wouldn't provide any evidence in this investigation. After all, there were numerous incidents already that should have generated something, but I was yet to capture anything paranormal. How things changed this time!

I rewound the thermal imaging footage to early morning and sat with a cup of coffee watching the screen. I noticed the figure of Christine walking up the stairs to Maggie's bedroom. I then saw her move towards the bedroom door and place her hand on the handle. As she did, I saw something else shift in the background behind her. Excited, I played the clip back, zoomed in, and realised it was the little boy! He seemed to be watching Christine as she walked across the landing, but as soon as she put her hand on the door handle, he instantly hid.

I placed a camera inside Maggie's room the previous evening, and so I could see everything clearly as her mother's heat signature entered the bedroom.. The door slammed behind her, and I watched the woman's temperature rise noticeably in the following few seconds which must have been when she experienced the rancid smell. Then I saw something else in the room with her. It was a much bigger figure.

Whatever it was seemed to rise up from the ground behind Mrs Evans as if it had been crouching, and then place its hands around her neck. I watched as Christine's body temperature increased again during a violent struggle in which the lady appeared to pass out. The large figure behind her disappeared without a trace the moment her body hit the floor. I could not believe my eyes, and I shouted John and Christine through to the kitchen to show them all the footage.

They couldn't believe what they were seeing either, and we must have spent at least half an hour watching the clip over and over. We zoomed in, reduced the speed, altered the contrast, and just about everything else we could do to get a better view of the figure behind Christine. It was easily six and a half feet tall, and as much as I didn't want to admit it, there was no doubt it looked somewhat similar to the evil man in the photograph sitting on the table next to me. I started walking over to the table to grab the image so we could complete a comparison, but it had disappeared!

Neither John or Christine knew where the photograph was, and thinking back, I don't think I saw it all day. All three of us went back into the living room to ask the girls if they'd moved it, but when we got there, both of them had disappeared too!

Once again we all bolted for the stairs with Christine leading the way and shouting the names of her daughters. There was no reply, and that only made us run faster. John threw the bathroom door open, but it was empty. I darted for Emily's room, but the girls weren't in there either. Christine opened the only door left on the landing and instantly began shaking, unable to speak a word, but clearly witnessing something traumatic. I gently but frantically pushed her out of the doorway so I could see inside. John was just behind me.

The youngest Evans' daughter Emily was sitting cross-legged on the floor of the bedroom, which still had the words "LEAVE THIS HOUSE" written thousands of times across the walls. She had both hands over her eyes, and the little girl was counting upwards as if playing a game of hide and seek. However, that wasn't the sight that was giving Christine a panic attack.

The oldest Evans' daughter Maggie was also sitting cross-legged. The only difference was that this girl was levitating in the corner of the room with her head only inches from the ceiling and her eyes rolled into the back of her head. All I could see was white when I looked at them.

John quickly tried to push past me and rescue his daughter, and although it took every ounce of strength I had in my body, I managed to stop him. I told the Evans' parents that something was in the room with their daughters, and it would likely injure them if they tried to intervene. Both Christine and her husband were in a state of panic, but they listened and allowed me to go into the bedroom alone. As soon as both of my feet were through the door, it slammed shut and I could smell the same stench that had been reported to me earlier.

"What do you want with these girls?" I asked the entity out loud as Emily sat on the floor and Maggie continued to levitate in the corner of the room. All of a sudden the entire single bed lifted from the floor to about two feet high which stunned me into silence. Then the wardrobe doors began banging open and shut violently. Emily uncovered her little eyes. "Ready or not, here I come," she said as the lights went out and the bed slammed back down to the floor instantaneously. I scrambled to find the light switch, but as I did, John and Christine burst through the door providing some much needed illumination from the landing.

Emily was still sitting safely on the floor near my feet and the bed looked undamaged, but I couldn't see Maggie.

"Where is she?" Christine cried out while frantically looking around the room. We thought we'd lost her for a few seconds until John opened the wardrobe and retrieved his daughter who was slumped over and unresponsive inside. Thankfully, she was still breathing, and all her vital signs seemed okay. The girl looked more sick than ever though, and I was beginning to think it would be sensible to arrange for her to see a doctor.

John carried Maggie, and Christine carried Emily downstairs. I was about to follow them when I heard a series of bangs coming from the loft. As I hadn't been up there yet, I made a mental note and decided that I would head up there with some recording equipment the following day. John had told me he didn't see anything up there when he looked, but I thought we could at least try to capture the noises using microphones. Who knows what else we might record?

When I did finally get downstairs, the entire Evans' family were back in the living room with Emily reading a book on the floor while Christine and John cradled their older daughter on the sofa. I asked if she was doing okay, but I was told Maggie's temperature was even higher than before, and she had begun to become delirious. She kept opening her eyes and speaking words that didn't make sense or seemed to be in an unknown language, and she was soaking wet with sweat. Both parents looked concerned.

Time was passing fast, and yet again we were all shaken and hiding out together in the living room into the early hours. There were noises coming periodically from all over the house, and the lights would cut out and turn back on every half an hour or so.. Maggie continued to look increasingly unwell. Her face was now a sort of grey colour, and the outbursts of unfamiliar words coming from the girl seemed to be more and more frequent. I was now certain her sickness was something to do with the haunting we were experiencing.

Just before I fell asleep for the night, I made the decision that things were getting out of hand with the Evans' family, and I desperately needed to call-in some extra assistance. I decided that I would get in touch with a friend of mine called Mark Wells the following day. He was once a priest but decided to turn his hand to other things in recent years. I thought he would be able to help as he had some experience with poltergeist cases through the church, and to be fair, there weren't many other people I could call.

I closed my eyes, wrapped a blanket over my head, and tried to block out the banging sounds and continuous outbursts from poor little sick Maggie for a few hours. It was very difficult.

THE POSSESSION

It was clear to me that Maggie was becoming very ill, and so I suggested to John and Christine they should ask their doctor to make a home visit. This case was ongoing during the global pandemic, and there were strict rules with regards to how many people could attend hospital appointments or Accident and Emergency departments. The Evans parents confessed to me they had not sought help already due to the fact they were scared of catching something in the hospital. So, both John and Christine were thrilled with my idea, and they arranged for the doctor to visit that same evening.

I spent most of the morning at Maggie's side. She was drifting in and out of consciousness, and she kept having those strange outbursts. I realised there was some kind of pattern to the noises, and so I recorded three different samples to see if I could make any sense of the words when I listened back.

Having read about and investigated many hauntings in my time, I know it's sensible to begin as simply as possible when attempting to determine the solutions to paranormal problems. I wanted to find out what Maggie was saying and where the words might be coming from. The first step I took was to reverse the audio and listen to the sounds backwards. Unfortunately, that didn't provide any interesting results. However, when I decreased the speed of the audio of all three samples by 250% and removed all the bass from the recording, I heard something that scared me to my very core. Maggie wasn't spouting nonsense at all. Far from it. In fact, the soon-to-be teenager was just speaking very, very quickly.

I alerted John and Christine to my findings, and they gathered around me in the kitchen to listen to the edited audio sample in all its glory. There, as clear as day, for all of us to hear, was the eldest Evans daughter repeating the words "LEAVE THIS HOUSE OR YOU WILL DIE."

Again, my laptop turned itself off without warning seconds later. That was becoming somewhat of a common occurrence during this case in Birmingham.

John left the house for a couple of hours to take his youngest daughter Emily to stay with her grandmother. Myself and John both felt it would be wise to keep the little one out of the way while the activity was so strong and dangerous, and as it happens, that was the last I would see of her (although I am assured little Emily is doing just fine these days.)

Removing the youngest Evans' daughter from the situation would mean fewer chances for contact with the entity of the little boy who loved to play hide and seek with her, but that was a price worth paying. I wasn't exactly certain the interactions were harmless, and until we fully understood the nature of the haunting and why the little boy was hiding from the evil old man, it made sense to send Emily away.

Maggie had to stay put because she was in no fit state to leave the house and her symptoms seemed to be getting worse by the day. I had a niggling suspicion that she might be suffering at the hands of the malevolent ghost, demon, or whatever it was, that continued to engage in violent attacks in the upstairs bedroom.

Christine asked me if I'd managed to get in touch with my friend yet at around lunchtime. I'd forgotten all about making the phone call, and so I quickly grabbed my mobile and searched through the contact list for Mark's number. He answered in less than three rings with the strangest remark - "I had a dream about you last night."

Once we were finished with the usual pleasantries, I explained the situation at the Evans house and asked if he could possibly come to our aid or at least take a look around and offer some advice. My old friend Mark told me the Church had been in touch with him only a week previously to ask for his assistance in a case of stigmata, and that he told them the same thing he was going to tell me: he wasn't interested.

Thankfully, I had a bargaining chip the Church didn't have, and that was a longstanding friendship. I'm not saying he didn't take some convincing because the phone call went on for more than two hours, but by the time I pressed the red button on my handset and sat back down in the living room, Mr Wells was on his way to us.

He would arrive ten minutes after the doctor, who checked Maggie's vitals, made some assessments, and determined she needed to see specialists at Birmingham Children's Hospital. He said there was no immediate danger, but if she were to take a turn for the worse, her parents should take the girl to any local hospital right away. Otherwise, all they had to do was wait for their referral letter. It was bittersweet news because knowing Maggie was okay was somehow soured by the fact I believed something paranormal might be attempting to enter her body.

It didn't take long for me to get Mark up to speed on all the events that had happened so far in the Evans house. You might think he would have been a little skeptical, but this man has known me for years, and he had no issue distinguishing between my serious and non-serious tones. Alongside that, banging noises began coming from the upstairs of the home again just as I finished explaining the situation, so it was pretty clear something was genuinely going on.

John and Christine needed a break. John had taken the day off work to look after his family, and he spent most of it cradling his daughter Maggie in the living room. Christine slept on an airbed on the floor at his feet. Both of them looked shattered.

Mark suggested we should allow the family to remain in the lounge and rest all evening while we do some exploring and hopefully encounter the entities. I agreed it would be a good idea, but just before we went upstairs, Maggie began making those noises again. They were exactly the same as before, and so I knew what she was saying. I told Mark who had a look on his face as though his brain was reaching the same conclusions as me - the girl was becoming possessed. "She's going to need some help pretty soon," he said to me. "I know," I replied.

Mark and I ascended the staircase as the banging, which was clearly coming from the loft above our heads, began to intensify.

I could also hear a scratching sound coming from inside Maggie's room again, and so I told Mark about how the girls were getting the noise to stop by simply asking politely. He questioned me as to whether or not I told the girls that was a bad idea, and I admitted I hadn't.

As both myself and Mark know all too well, demons and malevolent spirits often look to possess a soul when attempting to break into this world. It's usually a child, and that child is usually a pre-teen female. The entity can't take possession of the soul without being invited in some way. Or at the very least, the monster requires some form of interaction from the victim to enter their body. That meant it was more than possible that Maggie conversing with the scratching noise coming from behind the wall in her room could have opened the door that allowed the evil presence to come inside.

Being as I hadn't been up inside the loft at all yet, and nobody had ventured up there since John poked his head through the hole a week ago, Mark told me to fetch the ladders. I positioned them directly under the loft hatch, and we flipped a coin to see which one of us would climb the steps and open the hatch. I called tails, and I lost.

Standing with my feet half-way up the ladder, I reached out with my hands and managed to lift the loft door a couple of inches. It was just enough for me to shift my balance and push the door over to the side to gain access. "Good luck," I heard Mark say from behind me as I took a few more steps and my head popped up inside the loft. It was very dark up there, and I couldn't see a thing, but still the bangs were coming thick and fast.

I asked Mark to hand me the torch in his pocket and he turned it on before slapping it into my waiting hand. I cautiously lifted the torch into the loft and scanned it around to see what was up there.

Over to my left there were lots of boxes, presumably containing old toys, Christmas lights, that type of thing. To my right I could see boxes and boxes of paperwork which I gathered would have been Christine's student materials and documents relating to John's work. I then turned the torch to point directly in front of me and illuminate the length of the loft. It seemed to be largely empty except for a wooden crate sitting smack bang in the middle of the space. That was where the banging noises were coming from, and incredibly, I could see the box moving!

I quickly climbed all the way into the loft, and Mark made his way up the ladders too. Both of us stood there in the darkness with only the light of Mark's torch pointing directly at the wooden box which appeared to be bouncing on the floor. It would rise up a few inches and then make a loud thud every time it fell back down to the surface.

As any seasoned paranormal investigator will tell you; things never move on their own. If you are involved in a haunting case with elements of poltergeist activity and items are moving around, it's pretty certain that an entity is in the room moving the objects. I suppose it's just how these evil spirits try to scare the living, but in some instances, these beings can also move things around in an attempt to warn people or tell them something. It was vital both Mark and myself kept an open mind at this point.

Mark stepped forwards into the light of the torch and placed his foot firmly on top of the wooden box. This action seemed to prevent it from moving and making the loud banging noise which felt like at least some progress. I knelt down and carefully removed the box from under Mark's shoe. We wanted to take a look inside straight away, but decided it would make more sense to get out of the loft. I descended the ladder first with the wooden box in hand and Mark followed closely behind.

We didn't want to bother the Evans family, and so we opened the box without asking their permission. Given the circumstances, and considering the whole family was running on empty, I don't think we crossed the line.

Inside the box I found the photo frame that had gone missing from the kitchen table the previous day. It was facing downwards and so I turned it over to reveal the scary old man's face staring back at me. "He looks a bit menacing," Mark said, seeing the image for the first time ever. "Have you tried finding out who it is?" He asked.

I explained to Mark that Christine had been in touch with the charity shop where she purchased the photo frame, but they weren't able to tell her where it came from. Mark looked at the picture for a moment before exclaiming excitedly "that's a mugshot!"

Unbeknownst to me, my good friend Mark Wells, being somewhat of a Birmingham history buff, had spent time researching in West Midlands Police's archives at some point in the recent past. While he couldn't guarantee he was correct. Mark was reasonably certain he'd seen similar photographs to the one in the Evans house before. He informed me images like that were some of the earliest mugshots ever taken, and he had a friend who worked for the police who might be able to shed some light on the matter. I asked him to get that sorted as soon as possible because if we could work out the identity of the evil man in the photo, we could potentially work out what was happening.

I closed the loft hatch and went downstairs with Mark to find Maggie, Christine, and John all fast asleep on the living room sofa. They remained there for the rest of the night while I showed Mark some of the footage and audio I'd managed to collect thus far. He was rather impressed and keen to get involved as he could see how much of a detrimental effect this was all having on the Evans family.

Mark told me he brought a Ouija board in his car that he would like to try the following evening if the family would consent, and I told him they'd probably agree to anything that might help at this stage. It was only then that my friend and ex-priest gave some details regarding the dream he had about me the previous night.

"You know why I packed the Ouija board?" He said as if building anticipation for the uncovering of a secret. "It was that dream I said you were in last night. You called me on the phone exactly as you have done today. I eventually agreed to help, as I have done, and then I came here and we found the photograph in the loft. All the events in my dream played out precisely as they have done today. What's weird is, I woke up with an image in my head. A really simple logo-type thing. Like a bull's head in a circle? I think maybe it has something to do with the seance, but we'll find out about that tomorrow, I suppose."

I was stunned. The things happening around me were so crazy I didn't know whether to believe my own eyes, and now a dear friend I roped into the investigation was having premonitions about the Evans family and the attempts we would soon launch to battle their otherworldly tormentor. Needless to say, I needed a drink, so I poured myself and Mark a glass of whiskey and made up the sofa bed before calling it a night. Mark decided to stay up and keep watch while taking another look through the thermal imaging footage, and as you will soon see, it was a very good job he did.

THE SEANCE

Mark shook me awake excitedly at around five o'clock in the morning. He'd clearly seen or discovered something, and without a word, so as not to wake the Evans family, he quickly dragged me into the kitchen. "I've found it!" My friend and new assistant said with a look of accomplishment on his face. I didn't know exactly what Mark had found, but as my eyes began to focus on my laptop screen, I could see a paused image from one of my thermal recordings.

Mark informed me that we were looking at a still frame from the video taken a couple of evenings previously in Maggie's bedroom. The frame was from around ten seconds before Christine entered the room and felt hands around her throat. At first I couldn't see anything unusual, but then Mark pointed towards the top left-hand corner of the screen. There was a face! And not just any face!

I picked up the box we retrieved from the loft the previous evening and opened it up to find the wooden photo frame with the photograph of the evil old man still inside. I held the picture up to my laptop screen for comparison and my initial suspicions were confirmed straight away. The faces matched exactly. We now had evidence that proved that the malevolent entity in the Evans house was, in fact, the scary-looking old man in the photo! What's more? We also believed the image was an early mugshot from sometime in the 1800s, and if that was the case, we would definitely be in a position to identify him with a little research.

Finally the pieces were beginning to slot into place, and all we had to do now was get in touch with Mark's friend at West Midlands Police to ask if we could take a look through their records. If this particular photograph was a mugshot, the Police should at least know the man's name and which crimes he committed. I hoped that would be enough to give some insight as to what might be going on and why he was haunting the house.

Myself and Mark were attempting to be quiet as it was still early and the sun was yet to rise. However, the three members of the Evans family asleep in the living room were woken rudely at ten past six by water dripping onto their heads from the ceiling. John jumped up first and darted up the stairs as fast as his legs could carry him, and Christine attempted to move her daughter Maggie to a dry chair in the corner of the room as the sofa was not soaking wet. While it wasn't exactly pouring through the ceiling, the water was clearly doing some damage.

Hearing the commotion, Mark and I went upstairs to see if we could be of any use to John, who instantly flew into a rage and accused us of leaving the taps on in the bathroom. It seems John wasn't much of a morning person, but as soon as we explained that neither of us had even been inside that bathroom, he soon calmed down. He did, however, swear blind that he'd definitely turned the taps off correctly the previous afternoon. We put it down as a simple mistake, but from this moment on, all the taps in the Evans house would turn on from time to time without anybody touching them. It wasn't the weirdest or scariest thing happening, but it's still worth mentioning.

Mark spent the rest of the day trying to get in touch with his friend at West Midlands Police, and I took some time out to explain our seance idea to Christine and John. As I expected, they were more than willing to give it a try, and thankfully Maggie looked a little better that day. She was still drifting in and out of consciousness, but her cheeks seemed to have a bit more colour than they had before. It was enough to convince me she was strong enough to endure any challenges the seance might bring.

We all ate dinner together, and then I prepared the Evans' living room for our ceremony. I closed all the curtains, grabbed the table and chairs from the kitchen and put them in the middle of the room, and I also lit some candles. Before we all sat down to begin, I set up the Ouija board that Mark retrieved from his car and placed an audio recorder on the table. We all sat down and joined hands.

I am not a religious person myself, but Mark used to be a priest, and so he performed a blessing and said a prayer. I instructed everyone to then place two fingers each on the planchette which was positioned in the middle of the Ouija board.

"Is there anybody there?" I said after making a quick decision to take the lead. Mark repeated, "is there anybody there?"

Nothing. The flames of the candles didn't even flicker, and so we tried again. "Is there anybody there?" I said.

A few seconds later we got our reply, but it didn't come from the planchette on the Ouija board as we expected. Much to our horror, the reply came straight from the poor Evans daughter Maggie, whose eyes were rolling into the back of her head. "I'm here!" She said in a deep and gritty voice, more suited to an old man than a little girl. .

John and Christine both looked to me for reassurance, but I

couldn't give them any. All I could do was continue. "What do you want with this family? Why are you in this house" I asked while looking over towards Maggie who was sitting directly opposite to me.

"She brought me here," the little girl replied sharply in the same gruff voice while pointing at her mother.

"Don't you think it's time to go from here and leave this family alone?" I pressed further, hoping to talk some sense to the spirit. "I'm not leaving without my boy!" the voice shouted violently.

Just at that moment, all the candles went out in the Evans' living room, and we found ourselves in complete darkness. I told everyone not to panic and I could hear John attempting to find the matches. The room was pitch black for around ten seconds, and when John lit a candle, it was worryingly clear our party of five had somehow turned into a party of four. There was an empty seat across the table from me. Maggie was gone!

We would have started running around the house trying to find her straight away were it not for the fact we were all witnessing something else that left us frozen in our seats. The Ouija board was still laying on the table in front of us, but the planchette was far from still. It was moving around the board frantically at considerable speed, and it once again appeared to be spelling out the words "LEAVE THIS HOUSE."

After a few seconds, the planchette flew off the board and hit the wall behind my head. That brought us all back into the moment and made us realise we really needed to look for Maggie.

Mark stayed downstairs while myself, John, and Christine checked upstairs. We could not find Maggie anywhere, and we were all starting to become worried. She only had about ten seconds to leave the table when the lights were out, so we didn't believe it possible she could have gone far. Then just as we were about to give up hope, Mark began shouting from downstairs "I think I can hear her!"

We ran down the stairs and into the kitchen to find Mark standing with the pantry door open and his head leaning inside. "She's in here somewhere" he said, "listen!"

All four of us then heard the sound of Maggie, in her own voice, calling for help. John started ripping away at the shelves, removing everything he could from the pantry. Christine shouted to Maggie and told her to keep making noise so we could find her. Once the pantry was empty of food, it was pretty clear Maggie wasn't in there, but we could still hear her calling for help. Having a light bulb moment, I stamped my foot on the floor of the room, and it made a kind of echo noise. Like there was a space underneath. "Maggie must be down there," Christine said as John ran to fetch his tools.

While the Evans family had lived in their home for many years, it seems they were unaware that the floor in their pantry was false, and that there was at least some kind of space underneath.

John returned with his toolbox and used the claw of a hammer to lift the floorboards one by one. In doing so, he slowly revealed his frightened daughter who was cowering underneath and seemed to be standing on a brick staircase. I lifted Maggie out of the hole and passed her backwards to Mark and then Christine. She looked okay all things considered, but none of us had any idea how she could have possibly ended up in such a crazy place. It would have been impossible for the girl to get there herself, and so as unbelievable as it may seem, I am left with no choice but to accept she must have been put there by something otherworldly.

John continued removing the floorboards in the pantry to reveal a staircase made of red brick that had no less than twelve steps leading down and under the house. I asked John if he knew his home had a basement, and he just shook his head. "There's no basement on the deeds," he said. Mark then suggested we go down and take a look, but Christine wanted us all to stay together, and she didn't want to leave her daughter Maggie. So, after some discussion, it was decided that myself and Mark would go down the staircase alone while John remained with his family.

I'll be honest and tell you that the walk down those stairs was perhaps the scariest of my entire life. The bricks were old and crumbling under my feet, but they held up long enough for me to get to the bottom safely and ask Mark to pass his torch. I flicked the switch and shined the light around from left to right. This wasn't any coal store or small basement you might expect under a house in Erdington. Far from it. The Evans family had an entire room down there that spanned the width and breadth of the house, and it looked spooky as hell.

In front of me were nine red brick pillars which appeared to prop up the foundations of the property. The floor was thick with dust, and I don't personally care to remember the size of the spider webs, but they were big and they gave me chills. Mark and I explored the space and soon noticed some markings on a wall at the far end of the room (which would have been underneath the front wall of the house.) As we moved closer with our eyes squinting because of the dusty air, I began to think we were looking at a pentagram. However, I soon learned I was probably wrong when I heard Mark shout "Bingo!"

The symbol on the wall was a red colour, almost like blood, and Mark instantly knew it was the one from his dream. It was made up of a circle which surrounded the head and horns of what looked like a goat in a very pentagram-style. I knew I'd seen it before in some book on the occult, but I couldn't remember what the symbol meant.

Just then, there was a rumble and the ground began to shake. It felt like an earthquake which almost knocked us off our feet. There was dust falling from the floorboards above our heads, and for a split second, I really thought the house was going to fall down. Alongside the tremor was a deep growling noise that appeared to be coming out of the darkness at the other end of the basement. Needless to say, neither Mark nor myself hung around. We ran back up those old brick stairs as fast as our legs would carry us, and we were met in the kitchen by a somewhat bemused John and Christine.

"What's all the shouting about?" John said. "We were just coming to check you were okay."

A little unsure as to why our shouting seemed confusing to them,

I asked John and Christine if they had just felt an incredible earthquake to which their replies were both negative. Mark and I were now confused. The tremor we had just experienced in the basement should have been recorded miles away, and yet none of the three members of the Evans family still residing in the house above us felt a single thing. I don't have any explanation for how that could be possible, but it happened.

It was decided that the basement was now officially off limits for the rest of the evening, and John would arrange to have some specialists go down there and check the foundations were safe as soon as possible. He would also contact the council to find out how it would be possible for him to have a basement that is not recorded on the blueprints for his property.

Maggie was fast asleep on the sofa with her parents when myself and Mark finally sat down close to midnight. She looked very unwell, much worse than she did earlier in the day, and that made me question how much more she could take. Were we putting her at too much risk by effectively allowing the poltergeist to use her as a conduit? I hoped not, but I also knew we'd better solve this problem and end the haunting soon or that little girl would be scarred for life.

THE OLD MAN

It was now 6th October and I'd been living at the Evans house for almost one week. Things were seriously heating up, and it felt like my investigation was finally going somewhere. We'd managed to identify the evil presence in the property was indeed the scary man from the photograph that couldn't be thrown away or destroyed. We also held a seance where the entity had taken control of the Evans daughter Maggie and told us he wouldn't leave without his boy, who was presumably the small ghost child who had been making contact with the youngest Evans daughter before she left to spend time with her grandmother. On top of this, we now knew there was a previously undiscovered basement under the house that contained some pretty weird symbolism.

I have to be honest and tell you that I was expecting a hidden camera crew to jump out and tell me it was all a prank for some TV show, but that never happened. This was real. It was frightening. And if we didn't expel the spirit from the house soon, young Maggie might never recover. Considering all this, I was thrilled when Mark ran into the kitchen shortly after I awoke to tell me he'd just got off the phone with his friend from West Midlands Police, and they were going to help us!

According to Mark, his friend had full access to the WMP archives, and he could check our photograph against all the mugshots in the entire system, even those from a very long time ago. Without wasting any more time, Mark took the picture of the evil man from the kitchen side and snapped it with his smartphone camera. "That'll do," he said before emailing it over.

As it was still rather early, Christine and Maggie were fast asleep on the double sofa bed in the living room. John, unfortunately, had to go to work, and so he was out of the house all day.

I woke Christine up gently with a coffee and a slice of toast. I was so excited about potentially identifying the man in the photograph that I just had to tell her all about it. She seemed thrilled that we were making some progress, but I could tell this whole ordeal was really taking its toll on the Birmingham mother. There were dark bags under her eyes, which rarely shifted from looking at her sick daughter for more than a few seconds.

The taps were still turning themselves on periodically, and so myself and Mark took the responsibility of checking them all once every hour. There were also a lot of noises coming from the upstairs of the house all day, but after the events of the previous evening, I think we all decided it was best to ignore them as much as possible.

Maggie spent most of her time knocked out on the sofa bed, but she would awake every so often and speak in the most unusual of tongues. She had progressed from simply saying the same words over and over at high speed into some other form of language. I recorded it as much as possible, but even as I sit and write this book today, nobody has ever been able to determine what the girl was saying. Maybe it was nonsense? It's possible, although I suspect it wasn't.

Alongside the changes in Maggie's outbursts there was something else that had me very worried. I wasn't sure exactly what was happening because it only occurred when nobody else was in the room, but scratches began to appear on the young girl's body, specifically in the stomach area. Either the malevolent entity was hurting her or Maggie was hurting herself, but this was an escalation nobody wanted to see.

Christine decided to put woollen gloves on her daughter's hands to limit the opportunity for Maggie to injure herself, and she also wiped an antiseptic gel all over her stomach to ease any irritation caused by the scratches. After she'd done that, the distraught mother called myself and Mark into the kitchen.

"I can't take any more of this!" She said while breaking down in tears. "This just isn't fair. Why is this happening to my family? You two said you were gonna help, so help? Please get rid of this thing, I'll do anything."

I reassured Christine that everything was going to be okay, and that we would know exactly what we were dealing with and how to get rid of it very soon. She didn't look convinced, and I can't really blame her. All this was happening to her family and she couldn't even ask her friends for help. She couldn't ask anyone other than me. Nobody would believe her and she'd be humiliated. I understood all too well the emotions she was feeling.

Mark's phone began to ring, and I've never seen someone press "accept" so quickly in all my life. It was clearly his friend from West Midlands Police, and by the sounds of things, it seemed as though he might have had some luck during his search. I eagerly waited at the kitchen table with Christine as Mark took the phone call outside. He returned five minutes later with a smile on his face.

"I've got two words for you," he said. "Isaac Ellery."

As that name came out of his mouth the entire atmosphere in the room changed. I felt the hair standing up on the back of my neck and a chill go down my spine. The light seemed to dim considerably even though it was the middle of the day, and all three of us heard heavy, uncomfortable breathing coming from the living room.

We ran to check on Maggie only to find her suspended in the air in the crucifixion position with her eyes rolling into the back of her little head. I ran towards her and put my arms around her body but was instantly thrown back against the wall by some unknown force. I believe I was unconscious for a moment, but I regained my bearings just in time to see Mark fly across the room and hit another wall hard. Christine was frozen solid, completely unable to move for a moment before collapsing on the floor.

Just as she had done the previous evening Maggie began speaking in a deep, gritty Birmingham accent, "If you don't give me my boy, I'll take your girl." She then let out the most bloodcurdling scream I've ever heard. It sounded as though she was being tortured to death, and I believe the entity inflicted so much pain on her as a show of strength. It was telling us Maggie was going to die if we didn't hand over the little boy ghost, who was presumably still hiding upstairs.

Maggie then fell down to the floor with a thud as myself, Mark, and Christine all clambered to our feet and went to her aid. She was unconscious once more and appeared largely unharmed, but her mother was still terrified of what might happen if we didn't work out a way to satisfy the entity or somehow hand the little boy over.

A few minutes later, once we all had a moment to catch our breath, Mark began to tell Christine and I a little more about his conversation with the guy from West Midlands Police. Apparently, this Isaac Ellery wasn't just some random criminal from Birmingham, far from it. In fact, he had quite an interesting story that Mark repeated as best he could.

Apparently, the photograph of Isacc Ellery in the Evans' house was an original mugshot taken by West Midlands Police in 1853. It was thought to be the first ever recorded mugshot of a criminal in UK history, and because of that, the pic was actually quite famous among law and order history buffs. The contact at WMP told Mark they had a copy of the image in their files, but he believed the original went missing. Therefore, it was probable that the photograph in the Evans' kitchen was that original, and

Christine had inadvertently brought it into the house with her charity shop photo frame.

Mark also told us a little about the crimes of Isaac Ellery. While there was no record of him being involved in anything other than "cushion theft," for which he served seven years hard time in the work camps of Australia, there were a few interesting notes in his file. Allegedly, the arresting Police Officer said of Ellery that he was a "dangerous drunk," and that he was "known to beat his wife." The judge presiding over his case also called him a "despicable man of darkness."

Those sounded like really strong terms for someone whose only crime was stealing a few cushions, and I was pretty convinced there was much more to this man. That's when I had the bright idea of throwing the question out to the world. Now we knew the name of the evil-looking man in the photograph and some basic information about him, there was every chance we could find someone who knew more. So, I wrote a Facebook post in every Birmingham-related group I could find asking for people to get in touch if they recognised the name or the picture. I was convinced someone out there would know something, and I thought maybe he might even have some living relatives.

The afternoon went by without too much drama. Mark and I

checked the taps every hour, and Christine cradled her daughter on the sofa until John arrived home from work. We were quick to fill him in on the day's events and the information we managed to uncover.

I also spent an hour or so researching occult symbolism online to see if I could identify the image scrawled on the wall in the basement. After a lot of searching, I found it. The logo on the bricks downstairs represented a deity called Baphomet, which was once worshipped by the Knights Templar before being incorporated into various different occult and mystic traditions. In most instances, the Baphomet promotes balance, being half-human and half-animal while also being male and female. Experts believe the deity can also be good and evil, often at the same time, and so the presence of the symbol could be positive or negative. I hoped for the best.

I still had no idea why it was on the basement wall, but I was convinced the logo was relevant as that's where the entity chose to hide Maggie during our seance. It was almost as if the poltergeist wanted us to find it for some reason. I needed more time to think, but sadly, it seemed that time was running out for the Evans family. Maggie wouldn't survive much more of this, and I wasn't certain her mother and father would either.

After dinner and a few tap-checking bathroom trips, myself, Mark, Christine, John, and Maggie were sitting in the living room watching TV. We talked about anything and everything, and tried to block out the paranormal activity occurring all around us. The lights flickered, there were bangs coming from upstairs, and ever more scratches appeared on young Maggie's tummy - into which her mother frantically rubbed the antiseptic gel. I can't tell you what time everyone fell asleep because in my shattered state, I was the first to go.

THE TRUTH

The next morning I ate a quick breakfast before logging into my Facebook account to see if there were any comments on my posts about Isaac Ellery. It was clear the people of Birmingham were very knowledgeable about local history from the fact more than a hundred people had taken time to respond to my request for information. I thought the sheer number of comments was encouraging, so I sat down at the kitchen table next to the mugshot photograph and began reading through them all.

While all those Brummies meant well, I found myself increasingly disappointed with the first round of responses I read. Most of them only offered the same information I already knew, which is freely available on the internet as well as from the WMP archive. I scrolled and scrolled, then just as I was about to give up hope, I noticed the following message posted in reply to my request:

"Hi there. My grandad lived in Birmingham all his life, and I'm pretty sure his grandad used to tell him stories about this guy.

Drop me a message if you want."

I did want, and so I fired off a private message as fast as my fingers could type it. I asked if the gentleman in question was still alive, and whether it would be possible to get any and all information about Ellery. The reply came back only a few seconds later. "Sure, here's my number 078********."

I called straight away and spoke to Josh from Aston, which is an area of Birmingham that borders Erdington. He told me that his grandad was still alive, and that he would give him a quick ring and call me back. I eagerly waited by the phone all day, but there was nothing. I was gutted. Maybe Josh had got the man in his grandad's stories confused with someone else? I just didn't know.

The supernatural activity in the Evans house seemed to be getting worse by the hour. Just before lunchtime, the bangs, which were now coming from the walls both upstairs and downstairs, seemed to reach peak intensity. There was no real identifiable pattern to the banging, and I felt as though the noise was getting louder and more violent because we were nearing the final showdown. I knew that we had to take action as soon as we had all the right information, and I suspected that time was coming. I was right.

At around seven o'clock that same evening, I received a text message from Josh in Aston that told me to check my emails. That's when I read the following:

"Hi Lee,

Sorry, I didn't call you back. I couldn't get hold of him for ages, but I think you might be interested in what he had to say. So check this out, Isaac Ellery used to work with my great, great, grandad at the cotton mill in Birmingham in the 1850s. He was a bit of a strange bloke apparently, quiet, always kept to himself. Anyway, It was big news when Ellery was arrested and sent to the work camps in Australia, but it's what happened after that's kept his memory alive all this time.

According to my grandad, his grandad used to tell him a horror story about Ellery involving what people found when they ransacked his home after the conviction. The guy lived all alone in a wooden shack somewhere on Gravelly Hill, and when people went there to steal his possessions, which is what tended to happen when someone was sent to Australia, they found the body of a little boy who had been strangled. The group didn't report it to the police initially as they were committing a crime at the time and would have faced prosecution for burglary. Instead, they moved the body and told the police they found it somewhere else.

But that didn't stop the rumours going around the pubs, and everyone knew Isaac Ellery was an evil child murderer.

My grandad said he hopes Ellery died during his sentence, but either way, he doesn't think he ever came back.

Hope this helps!

Josh"

I sat with my jaw open reading the email and wondered whether it was acceptable to send a reply telling Josh that Ellery was back, but I decided against it. I thanked him instead for the information and for taking the time out to help me. I also asked him to drop me a line any time if his grandad were to remember anything else.

The story made perfect sense considering what we were experiencing in the Evans house. It was clear for all to see that the evil spirit haunting this family did not come from a pleasant human being, and he was most probably a child murderer. That meant the little ghost boy upstairs had valid reasons for wanting to hide from him, and I did not believe it ethical for us to simply hand him over. Who knows what that child's spirit might have to endure for all eternity if he's left with Ellery? I had a long conversation with Mark, Christine and John, and they all agreed with me. We would have to force this entity to leave, and it had to go empty handed.

Mark and I began to make a plan. This would require something special, something unique, something that neither of us had ever done before, and if we got it wrong the consequences could be deadly.

There is only one way to force a malevolent entity to leave a house, and that involves performing a complete cleansing of both the building and the family. This haunting was so intense that such a cleansing had the potential to turn into more of an exorcism, which is what Mark and I feared most. We prepared as best we could, and decided we would attempt to perform the ceremony the following day.

It was now around eight o'clock in the evening, and poor little Maggie was struggling to breathe. She lay on the sofa looking barely alive with chapped lips, pale skin, and scratches all over her body. Her parents both sat with her and continued to care for their daughter. Mark explained everything about the cleansing ceremony we planned to hold the next evening, but I doubt Maggie heard a thing. However, we believed it was essential for her to understand the process for the cleansing to work properly, and we hoped that somewhere in there the little girl was taking note.

As the evening progressed, it became apparent that we were all hearing knocking noises coming from under the living room floor. Knowing that meant someone would have to go back down into the basement to check it out, I suggested that I and Mark should once again bear the weight of that burden, and so armed with two torches, we headed down the brick staircase in the pantry to take a look.

The room felt even more eerie than it had done during our last visit, and just for a moment, I thought I saw something moving in the darkness. "What was that?" I whispered to my friend while repositioning the beam from my torch. Mark didn't say anything, but he lifted a finger to his lips and made a quiet "shhh" noise. He sensed the movement in the shadows too, and we both knew we were not alone. We followed the noise of the bangs until we were right underneath the living room of the house where they stopped completely. I saw something in the corner of my eye again, and my heart began pounding like it was going to burst out of my chest. We definitely were not alone!

In front of us was the wall featuring the Baphomet symbol that was still somewhat of a mystery. We knew what it was, but we didn't know why it was there or who painted it. Something felt different this time though, like the area had been disturbed in some way. It was then that I noticed something strange on the dusty floor under my feet. There was an "X," as if marking some sort of spot. It definitely wasn't there before. I looked at Mark and he at me. We both knew what was coming next. "Is there a shovel in the garden shed?" He asked. "Let's go look," I replied.

Mark and I climbed back up the crumbling brick stairs and I asked John if he could fetch me something I could use to dig in his basement. He was a handy guy, so thankfully he returned a few seconds later with what looked like a brand new shovel. I explained what we found in the basement, and I told both John and Christine that I believed it possible their house could have been built on the site of Isaac Ellery's wooden shack - the place local people claimed he would take children before strangling them. If that was the case, it might be possible there was some evidence under the basement. The Evans couple agreed to let me dig, and so Mark and I carefully stepped back down the staircase and under the house.

It still felt like there was someone down there watching us from the shadows, but whoever or whatever it was seemed content with simply observing our actions. We walked towards the wall containing the occult symbol and I knelt down on the floor right in front of the "X". With one hand I dusted all the debris away and discovered that particular section of the floor was not concreted. There was nothing other than dry earth, and so I began to dig.

As I did, the Evans family started screaming and shouting from upstairs. I sent Mark up there to find out what was going on while I continued digging, and just as he left the room I hit something with the shovel. It didn't feel like the same kind of earth any more, there was something different about it. I was hitting something hard, and so I put the shovel down and continued to dig out the soil with my hands, all the time being careful not to damage whatever I had found. The item was only a few inches long and wide, and I quickly realised I was looking at some kind of old tobacco tin that had rusted and decayed under the Evans house for many years. I was intrigued.

I pulled the old tin out of the ground as soon as it became loose, and stood up to take a better look at it with my torch. There was nothing of interest on the exterior of the tin as the label clearly rotted away a long time ago. However, it felt rather heavy, and I was convinced there was something inside, but decided it was sensible to take a better look in the light.

As I started walking back up the brick steps, I sensed something in the room with me again and stopped in my tracks. It was just then that the spirit of the little boy appeared out of the darkness for a single split second before vanishing in front of my eyes. What was even weirder was that I thought he smiled at me.

After the brief encounter, I rushed back up into the house to show everyone my find and hopefully learn about the cause of all the commotion. All four of them were in the living room, and they looked as though they'd just been through something traumatic. "What happened here?" I asked cautiously. Mark explained how John told him all the activity in the house intensified a few moments after we went down into the basement, presumably just when I started digging. By the time he returned upstairs, Maggie was apparently being dragged around the room by her hair as John and Christine looked on, completely horrified. Mark managed to wrestle her away from the entity, but everyone was still incredibly shaken.

Once everyone had time to calm down, I showed them all that I'd found an old tobacco tin in the basement under the "X" on the floor, and they watched intensely as I carefully applied pressure to the outer edge with my fingers in an effort to encourage the lid to pop open, which it did, upside down. A number of what looked like little white stones then fell onto the carpet in the Evans living room. Curious, I bent down to pick one of them up, and after rolling it around in my fingers for a few seconds, I realised I was holding a child's tooth.

THE CONFRONTATION

I bent down and gathered all the other teeth up from the floor, and following a swift count, I determined there were exactly twenty of them in the old tobacco tin. That is the number of teeth most people have during their childhood, and so I realised it could be possible they belonged to the little ghost boy. It all started to make perfect sense. That's why he got my attention and led me down into the basement, and that's why there was an "X" on the floor. These teeth belonged to him, and Ellery must have pulled them out before or after his death, probably as some kind of memento. Regardless of how they ended up there, the teeth were not in the little boy's grave, and I knew that could be the reason he wasn't at peace. I explained my theory to the Evans family and Mark who all thought it made sense.

We desperately needed to find out the name of the child those men found in the shack on Gravelly Hill back in the 1850s. Then we could look at burial records and determine if it was possible to reunite the pulled teeth with the rest of the poor little boy's remains. If we didn't achieve this, I was concerned that his spirit would remain forever trapped inside the house even if we managed to successfully cleanse everything and expel the evil old Ellery. I quickly typed out another email to my new contact Josh to see if he could try to jerk his grandad's memory. He was our only hope.

It was getting late, and none of us had eaten a thing since Christine made some sandwiches at lunchtime, so I decided to order everyone a takeaway. Young Maggie was in and out of consciousness, but her parents were determined to get some food in her stomach to give her strength for whatever tomorrow might bring. John recommended I order from Orient Kitchen, which he assured me would deliver the best Chinese in town. I asked everyone to write down their orders, and then I gave the restaurant a call. I went for crispy chicken with noodles in sweet and sour sauce, if you're interested?

Around forty minutes later the doorbell rang and I made my way across the Evans' kitchen. I opened the door to find a rather startled-looking young man who, instead of handing over the food, proceeded to ask me if I was okay. A little taken aback by this unusual interaction, I said "erm, yes? Are you?" To which the young delivery driver explained he'd just seen something weird in an upstairs window that had freaked him out. I asked what he saw, worried that perhaps the evil old man had spooked him.

The shaken guy told me there was an old man in the window, but that he was completely naked. Confused, I apologised and paid him a decent tip for the inconvenience before he left. It was only when I went back into the living room with the bag of food that I saw John walking down the stairs with a towel wrapped around him. Then it all fell into place.

"Did you forget to close the bedroom curtains when you were drying off after your shower mate?" I asked. "Because I think you gave the delivery driver a bit of a fright!"

John and Christine burst out laughing, which was lovely because everything had been so stressful for a full week now. It was the first time I'd ever felt real joy in their house, and I was more determined than ever that the laughter would return for this family permanently. After we finished joking about John flashing the delivery driver, and thanking our lucky stars he hadn't seen something much worse at the window, we all sat down to eat. Maggie's parents fed her while she lay on the sofa, and she ate much more than I expected. The food was absolutely delicious, I have to say, and although this book is not sponsored by the Orient Kitchen in Birmingham, I fully recommend them if you're ever in town.

After dinner we discussed the procedure for tomorrow again

and all agreed that the family would relocate themselves if the cleansing ceremony was unsuccessful. It was far too dangerous for them to remain inside the property with the despicable poltergeist, and Maggie really wouldn't withstand much more. John called his brother and arranged for the entire family to go and stay with him if things turned sour or we didn't manage to expel Ellery's spirit. Although we were all nervous, there was a sense of calm that evening. Sure the knocking and banging was distracting, but we all knew this terrible experience was coming to an end the following day regardless of the outcome. I suppose you could compare it to how a boxer must feel waiting in his dressing room before a fight. The calm before the storm, as it were.

My alarm went off at six o'clock sharp, and I got washed and dressed in record time. The taps were on in the bathroom before I got there, but that was nothing new. I felt a mixture of excitement and dread all morning. The tactics employed to keep my mind occupied included cooking breakfast for everyone, reading more online about Baphomet the occult deity, and removing all my thermal imaging cameras and microphones from the house. I had a lot of footage by this point, and I didn't really want to hang around after the cleansing ceremony later on, so I removed them all before transferring one to the basement. That is where we planned to take on the old man's evil spirit and banish him straight to hell (or wherever you might believe malevolent entities end up.)

Christine and John were visibly anxious all day. I don't think I saw John sit down for more than about twenty minutes the whole time. He was as restless as me, but chose to keep himself busy with little bits of DIY around the house. Most people don't think about this, but when a poltergeist comes into your home, things tend to get damaged, and the Evans' house was looking somewhat worse for wear.

My friend Mark left us for a few hours to collect some essentials from home. While he didn't feel the need to don his old uniform and go full-priest, he did think that a fresh change of clothing and a crucifix or two might come in handy. I was relieved to see him return to us at a quarter to six in the evening looking revitalised and ready for action.

Maggie was bathed by her mother and changed into a clean nighty. Her outbursts had been rather intense all day, but I believed she was strong enough to endure the next few hours. After a stiff drink or two, we all lined up at the pantry door ready to descend into the basement. I was the first to head down the long brick staircase and into the dark and creepy space under the house. Christine followed me, and Mark helped John carry

Maggie down. It seemed to make sense to perform the ritual in front of the Baphomet symbol, as that was directly above the area where I found the little boy's teeth.

Mark placed a chair against the wall and John carefully sat Maggie down. We used a battery lamp to illuminate the space, but it was still pretty dark down there. Maggie was conscious and looking scared, but her mother offered words of reassurance as we all stepped back a couple of feet. Mark told the young girl to remain in the chair and that everything was going to be alright. The Baphomet symbol was right above Maggie's head, and I wasn't sure if it would help us or work against us, but we had to see this through.

Mark lit some bundles of sage and passed them to myself, Christine, and John while telling us to start waving them around. Seconds later I began to feel a familiar rumble under my feet. The Evans family looked panicked, but I explained that this happened before when Mark and I were in the basement, and I didn't believe the spirit capable of bringing the house down. I hoped I was right.

Mark launched into a prayer, recited some Latin, and then proceeded to demand for the evil entity to relinquish its control of poor young Maggie and leave the house. As he did, the little girl who was sitting upright in the chair with her chin down and pressed to her chest suddenly flung her head back. Far from looking like the terrified soul she was a few moments ago, Maggie's eyes were now once again rolling, and she let out an enormous unholy growl as Mark continued to make his demands. He repeated the words over and over again.

Maggie's chair began to shake. Each of the four legs were bouncing off the dusty damp floor, and her snarls and growls became louder and more intense. The evil spirit was hurting her. She was feeling its pain as the holy man's words were starting to take effect. Mark repeated his mantra. The entire basement was rumbling, and it felt like the house above was going to come crashing down on us at any moment. Then my friend addressed the evil entity by name said the following words:

"Isaac Ellery, I command you to leave this girl in peace and go back to whichever hell is reserved for sadistic child killers like you."

Everything went silent. The ground stopped rumbling, the dust began to settle, and little Maggie no longer sounded like a wild animal. In fact, she was perfectly still in the chair facing forwards. Without warning, both the young girl and the chair she was sitting on began to rise into the air. Then Isaac Ellery spoke through her. "Give me the boy," the deep and gritty voice snapped. Mark said "no," and I then watched my friend fly across the basement at rapid speed and smash into one of the brick pillars like he'd been hit by a bus. The same thing then happened to Christine and John who both disappeared into the darkness. It was now just me and Ellery, and I knew I had to finish the job myself. I picked up where Mark had left off and continued to make the demands. The entity struggled. It could have gone either way, but when I reached down to the floor and picked up one of the crucifixes that had been inside Mark's pocket, the balance of power seemed to tip in my favour.

I held the crucifix out in front of me and shouted at Ellery to "go back to hell!" The floor was once again rumbling and the entire foundations of the house were moving. The rest of my party were regaining consciousness and climbing back to their feet just in time to see the Baphomet symbol on the wall behind Maggie begin to glow brightly. The little girl was shaking and fitting and screaming, and the hair on her head was now standing up as if exposed to static. Then it happened. She tilted her head upwards and let out one last long scream that was so loud I had to cover my ears. The chair she was sitting on came crashing back down to the ground and broke into pieces on the floor. The girl cracked her head on the ground and was instantly knocked unconscious.

THE PEACE

Four days passed before Maggie regained consciousness following the cleansing ritual. She was taken immediately to Birmingham Children's Hospital where she remained in the care of well-trained, specialist nurses for almost two weeks. Apart from some bruising and the scratches all over her body, the little girl didn't sustain any more injuries. The same can't be said for my friend Mark though. He broke two ribs and fractured his left ankle that evening, and he wasn't up on his feet again for about a month. Mark told me that although he loved helping me out, he wouldn't be answering any more of my calls for a very long time, and to be honest, I can't say I blame him.

Christine and John came out of the experience physically unharmed, but I get the feeling the haunting took a huge toll on both of them mentally. Christine still hasn't returned to her teaching job at the time of writing this book, and the whole family says John hasn't been the same since it all happened.

There are some positives on which it is wise to focus though.

Firstly, Isaac Ellery has not made any more appearances in the family home since we cleansed both the building and the eldest daughter Maggie. Secondly, both of the children appear to have made full recoveries. Although I never saw little Emily again after she left to stay with her grandmother, I am reliably informed she doesn't remember a thing about her encounters with the spirit of the little boy. It really could have turned out a lot worse for everyone.

About a week after leaving the Evans' house, I received an email from Josh in Aston who had managed to find some time to speak to his grandad again. He provided me with the name of the little boy who Ellery allegedly strangled, and from that information, I managed to find where he was buried and reunite the teeth with the rest of his remains. I won't give the precise details here as it's probably in bad taste, but he was ten years old when they found him dead, and his grave is not far from Gravelly Hill. Let's hope he can now rest in peace.

There was one problem when all this was over, and that was deciding what I should do with the photograph of Isaac Ellery. I knew it was now possible to throw the picture in the bin or destroy it without the worry of having it appear back inside the Evans' house, but it seemed a shame to do that. So, I asked Mark if he could contact his friend at West Midlands Police again and ask if he would be interested in taking the image and putting it back in the archives. He jumped at the chance, which was lucky for us because I really didn't know what else to do with it.

The police contact actually told us there was no record of the original photograph going missing, and so he was surprised that he could only find a digital copy when we asked. I met him in Birmingham City Centre and handed over the mugshot which I presume he then slipped back into the WMP archives. Nobody knows how it disappeared from there and ended up in the photo frame Christine bought from the charity shop, and that will always remain a mystery. Still, it's back where it belongs now.

I never really worked out who or what put the occult Baphomet symbol on the wall in the basement of the Evans house, but I'm pretty confident it helped us in some way when attempting to expel the entity from young Maggie. It's supposed to represent balance, and so it can be both a good and an evil thing. On that evening in October 2021, however, luck must have been on our side because it helped, rather than hindered our efforts. Anyway, it's long gone now as John decided enough was enough a few weeks after the haunting and paid some specialists to fill the basement with concrete.

So while most things have gone back to normal and everyone

involved in the Birmingham poltergeist case came out of it largely unscathed, nightmares have become a real issue for young Maggie. She recovered well from the whole experience, but her sleeping patterns are still massively disturbed to this day. The girl claims to be having the same nightmare over and over again, and while her parents are in the process of seeking a private therapist, I worry she has some internal scars that could never heal. Her bad dreams involve being snatched from the street and dragged by an old, scary man into a dark room before he puts his hands around her throat. You don't need me to tell you where I think those nightmares might be coming from. What's even weirder is that she says sometimes the old man tries to remove her teeth first.

I hope these dreams just represent an echo of her experience being used as a conduit by Isaac Ellery, and that they will, in time, fade from her little sleepy head. She is such a bright and intelligent child, and she really doesn't deserve to have any lasting mental or physical injuries from these events.

While I've had no reason to return to the Evans' house since I left following the ceremony, I have been in touch with John and Christine, and we've chatted at length on the phone. I made it clear to both of them that I am always available if they need any help or support, but as is often the case with people who go through traumatic happenings of this nature, I get the feeling they'd rather try to forget about the whole thing, and that's just fine by me.

So what does a real-life ghostbuster do when the poltergeists stop moving things around and the malevolent entities leave their victims alone? Well, I rented a caravan from a friend in Kent for a week and disappeared off the radar. I needed time to gather my thoughts and process everything I'd just witnessed. Even for someone like myself who deals with the paranormal often, the events of the Birmingham poltergeist case were really something to behold. I'd always been interested in being at the heart of a haunting like this, but I can honestly say that I wouldn't like to go through this particular experience again.

Will I continue to investigate and write about the supernatural? You can bet your life on it! If this case taught me anything, it's that you never knew when you might stumble across something incredible and life-changing, and so you've just gotta get out there and keep pushing forwards.

Unfortunately, all the thermal footage and audio recordings (barring a couple I uploaded to the cloud) were destroyed during the cleansing. So was my laptop and every single other electronic device on the entire property. Everything was just fried.

However, I do have a couple of mementos from this case to remind me of my time in the Evans' house. Mark was kind enough to let me keep the Ouija board we used for the seance, and though I might live to regret asking for it, the board resides on a shelf in my office. I also have the crucifix I picked up from the floor in the basement and used to help expel the entity from young Maggie. That's safe at home too. Who knows? Maybe this case will become so famous I can auction the items off one day and retire to some sunny Caribbean island? A guy can dream.

Whatever happens in the future, I'm almost certain to be dipping my toes in the paranormal pond again before too long. I seem to be somewhat of a magnet for this stuff, although I'm not sure why. Even as I write this last paragraph, I can see my email inbox filling up at the side of my laptop screen. Thirteen people have been in touch with me for help and advice so far today, and no matter how fast I reply, the messages just keep on coming. It's funny but most folks didn't know what to do when they saw a ghost or something weird started happening in their homes before. Now it seems everyone contacts me, and I think that's pretty cool.

Until next time...

AFTERWORD:

I would like it to be understood by everyone who reads this book that the family involved does not profit from this story in any way. If truth be told, I had to spend a long time convincing them to allow me to write this book about the things that happened in their house back in October 2021. They finally agreed to the proposal as a method of payment for the assistance I provided during the haunting.

As always, if you would like to get in touch with me for any reason, paranormal or otherwise, please contact leebrickleyauthor@gmail.com and I'll get back to you as soon as I can.

Map showing location of Minstead road on Gravelly Hill in Erdington, Birmingham – right next to Spaghetti Junction.

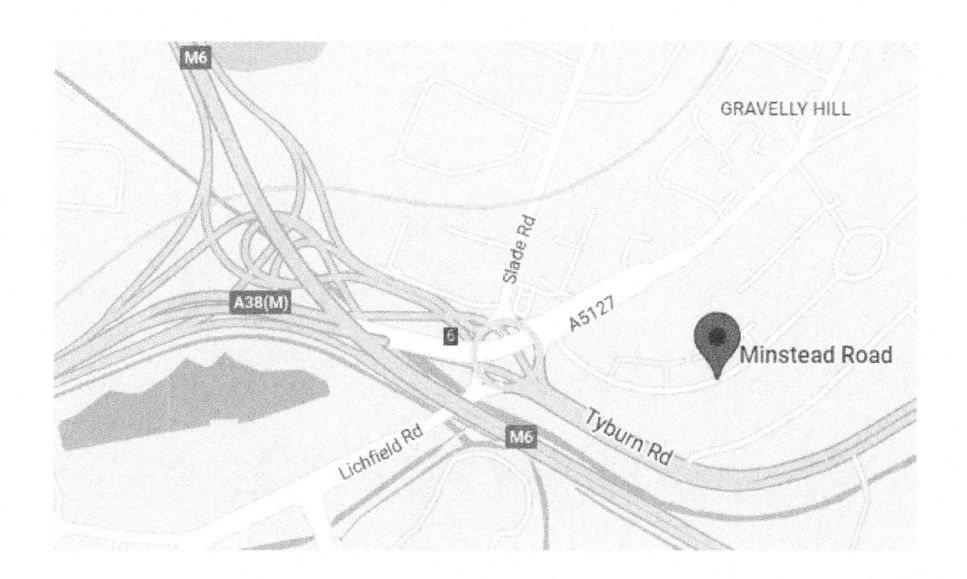

MORE BOOKS BY THIS AUTHOR:

ALL AVAILABLE FROM AMAZON

THANK YOU FOR BUYING THIS
BOOK AND HELPING TO SUPPORT
MORE PARANORMAL
INVESTIGATIONS AND RESEARCH!!!

YOU ARE AWESOME!

Printed in Great Britain
by Amazon